Step by Step

The Story of a Butterfly

It Starts with a Caterpillar

Shannon Zemlicka

Lerner Publications ◆ Minneapolis

Lerner Publications Company
An imprint of Lerner Publishing Group, Inc.
241 First Avenue North
Minneapolis, MN 55401 USA

For reading levels and more information, look up this title at www.lernerbooks.com.

Image credits: Prasert Krainukul/Getty Images, p. 3; Andrea Calispa/Shutterstock.com, p. 5, 23 (top right); Cathy Keifer/Shutterstock.com, p. 7; withthesehands/Shutterstock, p. 9, 23 (top left); JasonOndreicka/Getty Images, p. 11; Sari ONeal/Shutterstock.com, p. 13; CathyKeifer/Getty Images, pp. 15; 23 (bottom left); hwongcc/Getty Images, p. 17; Nicole Gilbo/Getty Images, p. 19; RyanKing999/Getty Images, pp. 21, 23 (bottom right); Vicki Jauron/Babylon and Beyond Photography/Getty Images, p. 22. Cover: CathyKeifer/Getty Images (caterpillar); Le Do/Shutterstock.com (butterfly).

Main body text set in Mikado a Medium.
Typeface provided by HVD Fonts.

Editor: Alison Lorenz
Lerner Team: Andrea Nelson

Library of Congress Cataloging-in-Publication Data

Names: Knudsen, Shannon, 1971– author.
Title: The story of a butterfly : it starts with a caterpillar / Shannon Zemlicka.
Description: Minneapolis : Lerner Publications, 2021. | Series: Step by step | Includes
    bibliographical references and index. | Audience: Ages 4–8 | Audience: Grades K–1 |
    Summary: "Watch a crawling caterpillar become a beautiful butterfly through
    colorful photos and simple, step-by-step text" –Provided by publisher.
Identifiers: LCCN 2019040497 (print) | LCCN 2019040498 (ebook) | ISBN 9781541597709
    (library binding) | ISBN 9781728401065 (ebook)
Subjects: LCSH: Butterflies—Life cycles—Juvenile literature.
Classification: LCC QL544.2 .Z47 2020 (print) | LCC QL544.2 (ebook) | DDC 595.78/9156—dc23

LC record available at https://lccn.loc.gov/2019040497
LC ebook record available at https://lccn.loc.gov/2019040498

Manufactured in the United States of America
2-52785-48361-2/23/2022

Look, a butterfly!

How does a butterfly grow?

A mother lays eggs.

The eggs hatch.

The caterpillar eats.

The caterpillar grows.

The caterpillar sheds its skin.

A shell forms.

The body changes.

The shell cracks.

Wings open.

The butterfly flies away.

Picture Glossary

caterpillar

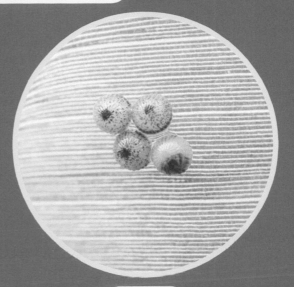

eggs

shell

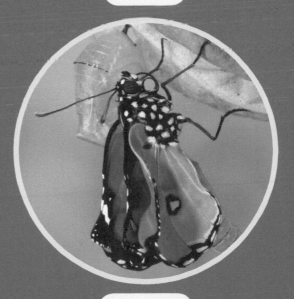

wings

Read More

Kenney, Karen Latchana. *Life Cycle of a Butterfly*. Minneapolis: Pogo, 2019.

Tonkin, Rachel. *Egg to Butterfly.* New York: Crabtree, 2020.

Zemlicka, Shannon. *The Story of a Frog: It Starts with a Tadpole*. Minneapolis: Lerner Publications, 2021.

Index